The Essential Dorothy Roberts

The Essential
Dorothy Roberts

selected by Brian Bartlett

The Porcupine's Quill

Library and Archives Canada Cataloguing in Publication

Roberts, Dorothy, 1906–1993
[Poems. Selections]
 The essential Dorothy Roberts / selected by Brian Bartlett.

(Essential poets series ; 17)
Includes bibliographical references.
ISBN 978-0-88984-410-0 (softcover)

 I. Bartlett, Brian, 1953– , editor II. Title. III. Series: Essential
poets (Erin, Ont.); 17

PS 8535.024A6 2018   C 811'.54   C 2018-900307-3

Poems from *In the Flight of Stars* are reprinted with permission of Goose
Lane Editions. All other poems are reprinted with the permission of John
Leisner, son of Dorothy Roberts, Pasadena, California.

Published by The Porcupine's Quill, 68 Main Street, PO Box 160,
Erin, Ontario NOB 1T0. http://porcupinesquill.ca

Copyedited by Chandra Wohleber. Represented in Canada by Canadian Manda.
Trade orders are available from University of Toronto Press.

We acknowledge the support of the Ontario Arts Council and the Canada
Council for the Arts for our publishing program. The financial support of the
Government of Canada is also gratefully acknowledged.

Canada Council Conseil des arts
for the Arts   du Canada

Canada

ONTARIO ARTS COUNCIL
CONSEIL DES ARTS DE L'ONTARIO
an Ontario government agency
un organisme du gouvernement de l'Ontario

Ontario
Ontario Media Development
Corporation

Table of Contents

Extended (1967)

The Self of Loss: New and Selected Poems (1976)

In the Flight of Stars (1991)

Foreword

Through the 1950s Northrop Frye wrote ten annual overviews of recent Canadian poetry for *University of Toronto Quarterly*. In the last of these, Frye paid special attention to two major books of lasting value, Irving Layton's *A Red Carpet for the Sun* and George Johnston's *The Cruising Auk*. Along with celebrating those two collections, he singled out another poet:

Perhaps the most distinguished of all this year's chapbooks is Dorothy Roberts's *In Star and Stalk*. This is poetry showing a unified imagination of unusual power.... In the background of her imagery are the free-wheeling rhythms of nature, the spinning earth and the setting sun, the stream of time that carries away the childhood memories of grandparents, the violence of storm and the fragility of birth. In the foreground is the image of the 'shell', the home occupied by the lonely and uncertain self in the 'almighty sea' of nature. Its products are the body itself, the house, and the stone buildings of civilization, the bus clinging to the white line of the highway.... What matters, of course, is the intensity with which these images are realized.

Frye's words *nature, earth, sun, time, childhood, self, house, body* compose a foundational vocabulary for discussing Roberts's work, yet a catalogue of passages embodying the archetypes suggested by such diction would hardly convey the distinctness of her sensibility and voice.

This undervalued poet was born in 1906, in the decade before the births of Canadian poets such as Irving Layton (1912), P. K. Page ('16), and Margaret Avison and Al Purdy (both '18), but a year after Alfred G. Bailey, two after Earle Birney and seven after F. R. Scott. Roberts's poetry was nurtured early on by a family environment including her uncle Charles G. D. Roberts and her father, Theodore Goodridge Roberts, who would publish several collections of poetry and over thirty novels. The first small gathering of her work, *Songs for Swift Feet*, appeared in the third year of the long-lived (1925–58) Ryerson Chapbook Series. She turned twenty-one that year, but much later she inscribed in a copy owned by her son, 'written before age 19'.

In several ways Roberts differs from most of the other Canadian poets cited above. Her style wasn't as recognizably contemporary as theirs, in terms of vernacular language, Modernist density, political directness or colourful personae. She wasn't part of any mid-century poetry movement; yet the family context, especially the lively letter-writing with her father and her painter brother Goodridge, was a different matter. Her long-term detachment from Canadian literary circles was understandable, considering both her living in the United States — Connecticut, New York and, primarily, Pennsylvania — for most of her adult life, and her long hiatus away from publishing poetry (her second chapbook appeared thirty years after her first).

More than any other Canadian of her time, Roberts wrote poetry of exile. Much of her imagination is rooted in New Brunswick sites and settings experienced in her youth, as she explains in 'Some Phases', a crucial introductory memoir to her 1976 volume of new and selected poems. The dominant currents in her poetry include feelings of distance from loved landscapes, memories of family residences and excursions, and the encroachments of time. 'Some Phases' states outright: 'The great upheaval of exile kept assailing me … rivers of streaming time and islands of the clung to and forests of finding what years had taken away.' Roberts also speaks of her eventual 'terrible need' to write poetry being connected to living in 'a country of exile', which was affiliated with the region most native to her but was also 'a country of time'. For Roberts exile wasn't only a matter of geographical relocation but also a psychological condition. The final paragraph of 'Some Phases' concludes: 'What I had lived in and left became an aesthetic world, but more: a home for the deepest inclinations now'.

The poems written by Roberts in her teens include the imagery of Pan pipes, ghosts, a faun, and a 'goose girl' destined to 'marry a king', but amidst the sentimentality we find the prophetic title 'The Exile'; 'Memories', which wouldn't be out of place in Robert Louis Stevenson's *A Child's Garden of Verses*, and shows awareness of memory's ability to 'sting', 'steal' and disrupt sleep; and 'The Jungle', an Alexandrine-lined, surprisingly violent sonnet, the speaker attacking dense vegetation but nature nightmarishly fighting back to reassert itself and bury the human colonizer.

In her maturity Roberts became a poet adept with fresh slant-rhymes (*weather/winter, simple/apple, down/form, God/cloud*), varied prosody and structure, and mixtures of tough-mindedness and tenderness. She is a poet attuned to the powers of anaphora, chanting and other sorts of repetition (see 'Early Morning', 'Rain Builds', 'A Pattern' and 'The Poets of Home'), and to synaesthesia (sound and sight blended in the lines 'Volume of green that if it sang would drown / All singers'). Roberts is a flexible poet of perspective, usually keeping what she calls 'my uncertain self' out of the dramatic foreground of her poems, yet still infusing her lines with the alertness and vocal registers of a deeply feeling person (as Frye wrote, 'What matters ... is the intensity'). She offers perspectives we might never have witnessed previously in poetry. From an idling passenger train, cattle in a nearby livestock train are sympathetically watched until the watcher suddenly, momentarily seems to become one with them ('Travellers'). Two swimming sisters experience the 'underwater strangeness' of watery transformation, then in future memories each is to the other 'a shape that never clears'. One of Roberts's later poems, 'A Marvel', begins with the memory of 'a galaxy seen through a telescope years ago', and from the perspective of 'where my life is now' that galaxy is recalled as — in one of Roberts's most spacious lines — 'small light blur becoming only in thought one of the great views.'

If Roberts is at times a poet of subjectivity, memory and mind, she is also often — sometimes simultaneously — a poet fervently attached to natural settings ('I had the green heart early', says 'A Son Enters Forestry'). The staunch, restrictive Protestantism of her grandparents' world helped compel her to write poems that foreshadow Alden Nowlan's early poems in a similar vein, but the 'cold' that both alienates her in its denials of vital energy and intrigues her in its association with strength and stoicism is complicated by the appearances of fire in her imagery. In 'Flower', she sees 'life as one flower', 'the whole world fresh, its fabulous ages / Turned back into it as renewing sap', and '[E]xtravagance of sex sustaining its fibres'. In 'Three Girls', a poem expressing frank sensuousness unknown in lines by the male poets of the Roberts clan, she describes girls undressing in a forest to feel the actual tactility of ferns and cedar branches ('To let the skin release its impulses / In little starts and pleasures'). The poem's final line removes any doubts that sexuality is connected to the sensuousness of the scene: 'Still is all lover's touch partly of leaves.'

Many more things could be said about Roberts's poetry. If I were to address a new reader of Roberts, I'd say something like this:

Why not compare her father's poems from his military years (poems often revealing bitterness and skepticism) to her 'Two Years', 'A Dance with Peace' and 'One', which speak of war in a mother's voice? How about spending hours over her longer poems, such as 'This Child' and 'The Great Activity of Death'? Be sure to check out the recent valuable essay on Roberts in Anita Lahey's prose collection *The Mystery Shopping Cart* (Palimpsest, 2013). Okay, apostrophes such as 'O inner earth', 'Come, winter', and 'O stars' (all from Roberts poems) were out of fashion long before her return to poetry, but rather than dismissing them as antiquated, experience them on a case by case basis for their tonal shifts, their pivoting effects. If you enjoy tracing influences, why not ask yourself if 'Movement' suggests Frost's briefer lyrics, or if 'The Shack' has roots in Li Po or other ancient Chinese poets? Dorothy Roberts deserves many eager, alert readers to engage with such suggestions, and to happily experience the pleasures of the poems.

—Brian Bartlett

Editor's note: The poems from Roberts's teenage years quoted here are from her early chapbook, *Songs for Swift Feet* (Ryerson, 1927). In an email letter her son, John Leisner, told me about her handwritten comment in his copy of that chapbook. The Northrop Frye quotation appears in his *The Bush Garden: Essays on the Canadian Imagination* (Anansi, 1971). Roberts's prose piece 'Some Phases' is found in her book *The Self of Loss: New and Selected Poems* (Fiddlehead, 1976).

The Jungle

I hewed out the heart of the jungle. Tendril and fern
And creeper were cleared by the cane knife: each in its turn
Crashed the vine-wrapped palm to my axe blow, and clump by clump
The bracken was beaten back, and the sap-wet stump
Was torn from its bed with the black earth clutched to its roots:
And the smothering growth gave way to the stirring shoots
That sprang from the seed I scattered so free to the soil.
A house green-thatched in the sunlight answered my toil.

I hewed out the heart of the jungle; and then, as I slept,
In on me, stifling, reclaiming, the lush tangle crept
To suck at the fruit of my work, cover and smother;
And over my roof the great trees reached to each other.

I hewed out the heart of the jungle. Close, ever close
Crawled in the vine and the tendril to smother my house!

Outburst of May

Volume of green that if it sang would drown
All singers; but it whispers — now the birds
Let it be heard for a little in the sun:

Soft hiss and shiver until through disks of light
The penetrating calls, fiery insistence,
Only the dove floating an easy note.

The evergreens extend in light-bright tips,
The vines fan on the wall, the roses show
A taut distension of their folded cups.

We in a telescope must be all green,
The flame of too much May. Fall, rain. Fall, rain.
From every surface starts the sound of rain.

May is the truth. To dampen down explosion
Autumn will have to come, the chilling fall
Of spent particulars before another tension.

Dazzle

Light looks from a dazzled leaf,
Stares like a small sun,
Glitters, and in the breeze
Leaps to another leaf.

Light speaks and the morning answers,
The surest answer from the tree,
Up, up, up, up and all open,
But the flight and the song breaking free
Of the branch answer, answer also,
And the brightest answer is the eye.

Light blazes from the car windshield,
Prints tendrils on the shimmering wall,
Twinkles in the flower cup—
Up, up, up, up
Answer the vine and the grassblade,
The squirrel and the ball out of sight,
Answer all the shapes broken up
Into shimmer and shadow. Light

Comes to the eye from the answer,
Not direct from the fiery core—
From the kindled pebble under the sprinkler
To the glittering eye
That answers with so much seen
And the blinded 'Why?'

Light plays with the chorus of the living
While the dead hurry down
Earthward to lift to the dazzle
Any answering form.

Cold

My grandparents lived to a great age in the cold—
O cruel preservative, the hard day beginning
With night and zero and the firewood
Numbing the fingers. God could have been in the flame
Responsive among the birch sticks, roaring
Up through the comforting pipes, and served all day
From the frosted woodpile, the continuing flame
As the sun almost let go of the bitter world.

But for them He stayed in the cold,
In the outer absolutes of cold among the fiery orbits,
And gave them the white breath and the blood pumping
Through hard activity stringing out the muscles
Into great age. They lived in cold
And were seasoned by it and preached it
And knew that it blazed
In the burning bush of antiquity
With starry flowers.

The Farm

My father was taken with the land
And after a long war
Came to it with a weather eye for bounty,
Praised what grew.

Trilliums, the painted and the simple,
Mushrooms round among the rainy crows,
And even the hard pebbles of the river
He cultivated like the knotted apple.

Following his quest within the living cycle
He served the ends of things in field and burrow
And quiet climb of spruce beyond the pasture.

Horses cost most to carry, traded down to
The weathered old one that his pity knew
And wouldn't sell for fear she'd turn to glue
And so miss out on heaven —

Heaven came true
Only when reached through earth. Soft-sounding rain
Raised the brooks loudly till the golden drought
Ran in the flood and with the striking cold

Brought benefits low, prized fragrances and texture
Downed to the root or stalk (but rose thereafter
And were as pink as ever in neglected pasture).

Prepared for the great blow, he raised a special
Expanse of radiance over the cold hill
Where gallop about in my diviner eye
The broken horses with their bits of gold.

Veranda Spinsters

If they are gone — and they must be gone —
The audience, and so the drama, is less.
Hot afternoon, elm-arched, brought their ensconcing
Of selves along the porch in odd best dress.

Eyes in a row veering to east, to west
Soon caught our coming with a stir of pleasure
Communicated to us till we stepped
More brightly into their expectant leisure.

In setting of shade and sunlight and old houses
We felt ourselves encompassed in a meaning
Beyond our presence — we were young, they seasoned
With summers and summers of this absorbent leaning.

Their thoughts expanding us, we bowed, they bowed
And their three spreading smiles grew vast, became
Applause which, remembered, fixes us again,
Focused in sunlight, into the town's frame.

A Dance with Peace

Coming in from missiles that proclaim their accuracy
Far off in another world, the army teaches
Also the deadly edge of the sudden hand.

Now my son shows me how he has learned to kill
With that hard edge — no sporty or crumpled fist —
Springing from secrecy with an animal growl.

One man would fall before him in the dark,
Or if resisting unroll
The terrible pattern of attack and defence
So intimate that it is almost love.

Here he performs for me the disciplined pattern,
Armoured only in his steely muscles, the bare blade
Of his hand flashing — the absence of any opponent
Being peace, and his young energy a dance.

A Son Enters Forestry

The trees by growing together can create
A mood all separate and imaginative,
An entering into something like a dream.

I had the green heart early—how cool it was—
But in the years forgotten almost, love
Could not take on that colour, money gleamed
Hotter than the sun, and everything was want.

After the season of your childhood—
In which your woods were fairyland for you—
I felt I'd lost you. Separateness set in

And would go on with manhood's stride accelerated
But that you found the forests again; and green
Is the one colour where we can now be close.

Green grow the surfaces of rocks to moss,
Green brims the air under the floating leaves,
Ferns find in inmost shade a place for graces.

And through you being here I can enter into
A man's forest of great trunks and towering heights,
A young man's wood of sudden stir and challenge.

The lost is here and now behind every tree,
The yearning like a green vine finds its way,
The subdued is a small orchid. All green grace

That stretches back through such bright history
Grows tall now in the care of you I cared for,
Kept from the world still for the world's refreshment.

Spokesman

Having little to say for itself
The stone stands up and speaks for all of us
Our deep desire to last.

Having no seasons within, its truths of weather
Are superficial and don't count beside
Our summer and our winter;

Therefore we chose it to address our heaven —
And it began at once to state our position
Reversed to terms more understandable

In castle and wall and column and cathedral,
In statue and simple tomb and mausoleum
And blocks of Stonehenge offering suggestions;

Goes on containedly against invasion
Deeper than rainy fissures, till persuasion
Makes us feel somehow in cold stone completed.

Companions

I saw seventeen gravestones
Form a small heaven
In a lonely place on a hill
Away from life altogether.

Their position one to another
Was of companionship,
And they used the wind among them
To whisper it.

I am the tongue now, said stone,
And I am the leaner
Close to another for reply
When the wind blows over.

Private

On our Sunday afternoon walk in the green woods
In the underbough damp and brown we found the fungi
Overboiling from a log of sooty rot

Into this orange, yellow, coral even —
But not made out of earth or out of heaven,
Not like the airy leaves or the earthy root.

Who will praise fungi on Sunday? — lobed like a brain,
Brilliant, of no airiness or rooted reaching,
But deeply composed with decay for a private sun.

Early Morning

The tool that is a stiff extension of the hand,
The light that comes slowly over the land,
The heat that lifts a sigh like a loosed soul,
The virtue that lies still in the log and coal,
The ship that holds a sail to the hard air,
The heavy shapes and their undoing in fire—

These find me in the morning and are sure
Of themselves in me, and me in them;
I do not know how else to have a day
That brings me out of the night and the uncertainty
And sets me up among things where I live.

By the soft hush of fire in the soul,
By the hard wind that shatters the personal role,
By the release of everything from dust,
I live in these hard things and the way they look,
I house my uncertain self in the star and stalk.

Bus into Night

We hang to the white line. We have an aim.
So have the cars flowing to us and away,
And the low cars that creep abreast and pass
With too much in the fastened hands that sway

The steering wheels an inch. So have the fields
Swept back in rows of furrows where dusk begins
To mount and overtake us. The line fades
A trifle as the dusk flows up and wins

A place beside the windows. Dimness fills
Inside with uneasy hurry, and the pace
Rattles as though quickened, loosens us from connections —
Till we are lost in motion when the race

Is won by this against us, this long dark
That seals us in, that stretches wide, that chases
Pale beams along the asphalt. Darkening motion
Dante could not have dreamt for us replaces

All destination, motion as circular
Taking our minds grooved for it. Oncoming lights
And passing lights wheel on as Earth in the dark
Follows a highway like her satellites.

Autumn Drive

The golden tree and the stream splashed with vermilion,
The man at the woodpile, the child pressed to the window,
We seize them and toss them away — we are like autumn —
We whirl them a moment in our sight, and then let go.

The grey farm buildings, the life grown from the mountains,
Beaten into mountain by weather that will never stop,
Even the grey farms are let go like asters,
Are held awhile in the years, and then let drop.

Plucked orchards and chilling fields we cast behind us,
Seizing, discarding like the wind, the frost.
The child at the window presses to watch our passing,
And when we are gone sees the leaves driven and lost.

The Gorge

By summer led we leave the golden heat,
The hot and shining surface of the land,
And climb down in, down rocks until we meet
Roots that find air as dank and still as sand.

Only their tips in leaning banks, the roots
Vein the brown air above the earthy spring
Bubbling brown, cold to circulate over rocks
That skeleton the soil. A covering

Of leaves is over air removed from sky,
The sunken air is watery to our breath,
The brown roots spreading, twisting round us tie
Us tight into our intimacy with earth.

O inner earth moulded of life and death
Where intermingled all thrust forth again
Into the blazing light, a flowery wreath
On all beneath, we bear your fragrant stain.

House in the Past

Sanctuaried in its sense of time-loss
The big house, standing silent and for aura
The beech grove; this we skirted many Sundays

To see the sun shine hard against the windows
And the old iron slave kneel by the doorway
Or, looking remotely on us from the carriage,

The ancient sisters go back to their haven
In the lost epoch—a family connection
Too remote to claim. We came here often

To feel this depth of time that we could acknowledge
Only in substance that our senses encountered,
The whole great sepulchre. Swallows into the chimney

Have come here since and circle
As I return at dusk; another circle,

Another ring of years is round the silence
Of that great empty house, one harder to pass through
Even than that before, a deeper aura.

Rain Builds

Rain falls above the hay
Hammering, hammering the slope of the barn roof,
Building a barn roof for the hay and us in the hay.

Rain parts on the peak and shapes —
Swishing — a barn for us
Solid in the drenched field,
Hammering, hammering.

Who'd know the shape of a barn
If it weren't for the rain
Hammering — parting at the peak —
Hammering, hammering?
Where would we be but wild in the open fields?

Rain falls over the scent of hay
Pressed to the peak and the swallow
And the dusty web
And stirred by us and the mice till we are drenched
In the dry sweet smell and the sound under the sun.

Rain builds around the hay, sluicing, a world for us
Separate in the lashed fields,
Hammering, hammering.

A Pattern

Severed from sociability the silence
Turns inward, sees the cold impersonal God
A stone, a still moon staying in a cloud,
And substitutes a pattern for the progress.

A pattern sits, a pattern says it's ready,
A pattern perambulates among its outposts
And colours all its doings with the fixed centre:

I have a farm of all the routes I've taken
That so absorb their place upon a hill
That they are birdcalls each from its location,

That they are branches setting up a system
Going down and down into a root and upward
Into a sun, and all alive with harvest.

A pattern rests, a pattern reaches plenty,
A pattern holds its seasons in assembly
And finishes itself in constant freedom.

I have a farm, and if things come together
In such a way as dancing, then I'll never
Find a more personal array of God—

A flower bursting forth, a flower spreading,
A vast array of stars, and apples hanging,
And corn and earth and sun, a flower falling.

Now That My Father

Now that my father is in his urn, and ash,
The frosty autumn leaves going twice to flame
Blaze in the trees and from their bright heaps flash
Back into light and heaven in his name.

I watch the expanding dusk burst into sparks
Of infinite burning; infinite too on earth
The slow combustion in the woods and parks,
In darting fins and wings and sleeping breath.

Rapid in him the light, as when a glass
Is focused full of fiery sun that leaps
Into a written paper, or autumn grass
Is snatched by fingers of the blazing heaps.

The bonfire of the setting sun has caught
The petalled tree, the dandelions have glowed
Away to puff of seed; my burning thought
Consumes its sorrow, knowing all form owed

To fire, to parting of the light and ash:
I loose a flame from burdening damp; it springs
Through leaves to air it coveted — oh flash
Like bird flown from a cage on frightening wings.

Two Years

Two years that keep my son away,
Two rings of the tree, two deaths of the flower,
And in the stone nothing to notice.

And in the castle by the shore
Where an event is kept preserved
Only, only the ocean's roar.

Time rests in stone, time speeds in petals,
Proclaims itself in turning wheels
Going round the earth and round the sun.
Over the ocean he is gone.

Time loses itself in hurrying squadrons,
And finds itself in petals fallen,
And rings him round in growth and knowledge.

I think of a castle standing always,
Censoring entrance of foreign powers,
Of all but the past's sincere admirers,

And looking out from its slotted keep
An ancient event. I think of water.

Before Marriage

Intolerably bright the thin
Saw-saw of the cicadas
And the moon, round, flooding in.

My daughter in my mind is flooded white —
No omen for her marriage but the bare
And piercing celebration of the night.

'Whose daughter?' shines the moon,
And the cicadas
Shrill on incessantly, insist, insist
None who are separate in their ways persist.

The heat is honey and the wind is lost,
The rain has never been, the vacant moon
Chimes with cicadas and the world is green.

Swimmer Returned

This swim has been too long, and now my foot
Touches at last on land, goes straining down
And touching sends the message of relief;
The mud stirs round the weed stems, bubbling brown.

The water drew me out. Its diamonds broke
Into my eyes. It snatched my breath with chill.
It swept me seaward struggling till my strength
Drained into current. It dissolved my will.

Lessened I come at last to mud and sand,
To my own element; washed up I wade
Through weed and lie full length pressing my wet
Flesh to the sand, and smell the leafy shade.

Panting I feel myself breathe in brief strength
From this support. I hear my easing heart
Seek its own earthly beat. Beyond I hear
Water of which I am a ceaseless part.

Sisters

My sister and I when we were close together
Clear to each other
Used to slide down beneath the river surface
And in a twist of current see the race
Of water break us from our sunny grace.

Wavering, shattered, glimmering each saw
No happy girl she knew
But underwater strangeness, shift and flaw,
Until the bubbles of our laughter drew
Us bursting up to the air.

Then we lay bare
And sure and shapely in each other's eyes —
We who no more to certainty can rise

But caught submerged in current of the years
See, wavering, each a shape that never clears.

Three Girls

The woods suggested it, the forest of urges,
And we undressed and walked among the leaves
To let the skin release its impulses
In little starts and pleasures lighter than real.

The delicate touch of woods checking the current
Between the flesh and world was most to be trusted
Of all the possible ways of coming to be
More than the personal triumph of the child.

Leaves, fronds, stones, mosses, brooks, tendrils and flowers,
I thank you for the delicacy of those hours
Letting the impulse out, the shower in
Of quick cool contact and the bars of sunlight.

Into the forest vanishing for persuasion
We found the dusky place and golden haven
Fern wand and cedar bough gradually gave—
Still is all lover's touch partly of leaves.

from This Child

(According to photographs of prenatal development)

2. Circuit

It's first made palpable by the heartbeat; plenty
goes on here, for the infinitesimal body
reaches as though itself the source of nourishment,
sends the blood out foraging in the placenta
that place of places, peace. This is the circuit.
This is the beginning of love.

As long as the heart needs to go out of the body
by the travelling road of the blood the course goes on here
voyaging round its circumference of intake and outlay
till the fingers are formed and the vision sealed in its splendour.

4. Progress

This child is more scientific
showing its veins in the quiet realms of the explicit,
networked all over in the route to be taken,
quiet child busy with the source of plenty
and shielded in its special self that is universal.
This child is more holy, having no sight and so seeing only
inward on the cells' progress to what is dignified,
hands, fingers, toes; and the past is forfeited
to each passage onward, front fastened over the heartbeat.

5. Grace

Organs hid have this outlet and it is the face,
and it is the fingers waving in their curled grace,
saying, 'I am whole here in my anatomy

having the most spectacular transports within me
of growth, growth into what is beautiful
if beautiful is a place'.
The face tells, and the fingers too, a sensitive lot
about life in the transparent sac,
how it feels, the ingrown shock and yet peace, bliss
of being the open sesame of internal force.
The face frightens the rest of the silent body
except the fingers that join it in being so expressive.

6. A Spell of Not Being Born

'There is nothing more to do here', says the child,
'but suck my thumb and wear my veil and wait
through a little thickening of the skin that covers
the vein, the nerve, the pate,
the whole fantastic personable apparatus
floating upon its stem like any flower,
unfolded from the thought, elaborated
to this my steadiest hour,

and open the eyes, unseal them of their wax
that they may see — oh alien mystery,
as everything was alien as it was done
till it had come to be'.

Provider

On the stem of the father the daughter: he took me at zero
To the farm he was thinking of buying far off in the wilds,
There in the frozen north it stood a weird world
Of itself with lamps in the kitchen behind the hot stove—
And there he was placed in position to be his own Word.

On the hill with the hollows surrounding and forests strewn wide
Stood the house, stood the barn, ploughed the footsteps
      through the white tide
Of snow decreasing, increasing under sun and high cold,
And into those elements melted my father of the world
And formed again hardened and extended in rein, plough and sward.

By the footsteps in snow counted deeply, in wind smothered over
Was caught the frame house to the barn, back and forth
      morning and evening
By lantern, by cold, by conditions quiet and eerie
Attaching the beasts to our hopes in their sun-chinked eternity—
Over the distance our passing more than back and forth only.

And out to the forest for wood that would waken our chimney
Billowing into the blue, we were gone. There were only
The fence tops between us and forests of dark melancholy,
But wind had made distance gigantic. We crossed it and followed
The faint road on into the depths where our white logs were piled.

Come, high stars, and find me as solemn as there in the forest,
My friends the white tracks in the snow, and find me as open
To anything coming and going, and grow me as welcome
There on the bough of all being in the great semicircle,
Come, Winter, and grow me again where my father once brought me.

Distinct

Over the pale fields
And the woods' dim grey
The night begins to fall,
I walk this way.

The stars begin to shine,
The woods grow black
Across the crusted fields
I break a track.

Sparkle of many stars
The snow lying mute
Distinguish all I need
To take this route.

Failing of Farms

Identifying oneself with farms
That are fading off the landscape, falling,
While overhead the moon is within reach.

The old mills crumble and the streams are falling
And as I climb the hill
It is to find more farms that are my failing
And orchards crotchety with fading wood
Where buildings set in antiquated logic
Maintain one kitchen light.
                              Such is identity
And nothing growing can wipe the descent out.

Movement

Now in the first faint light, our room unlit,
The first sounds of the birds are scarcely shaped,
But from the quiet trees a note, a note
Comes at the touch of light in dark boughs draped.

Lifted on silence still the notes increase
Each of its fullness. Light has found our mirror.
Together light and song in balance grow,
Spreading and soaring till our time and error

Gradually form, worn, clamorous and worried,
Take over house and treetop, seizing sway
Over the mind extended from its waking,
And all the ancient newness draws away.

Shadows and Snow

Put in a spell things cease for a while to continue,
but the moon continues and the sun
so the shadows continue
on the otherwise still land draped all in whiteness
that takes the shadow as the thing outlaid and meticulous
and the thing just as the shape for the shadow to grow from.
Shadow and light alone move here, the silence
creaks with the weight of the one force, cold,
over surface lifted so high that tips are the treasure
calling attention to a world
where shadows and substance join hands making shadow the more active
balancing its snow.
Contours are shadowy too and the wind that left them
leaves itself asleep in their form.

Midway

She was lost in the wood because a few leaves fell,
They fell and changed the pattern of the wood,
A wind rustled and a few leaves fell, yellow,
And she looked around and her heart thumped,
And there she stood.

Pools of light brightened a little where the leaves fell,
She put out a hand to one and the sun was good,
Good as it is when the breath of indirection
Mellows its light; but where was she in the wood?

She was lost and she looked around and her heart darted
Wildly for the light pools that perhaps would tell
Which way the sun and if the sun were followed
Where she would come to, where if a leaf fell
Right at her feet and yellow leaves were a pathway,
Where if a wind rustled and more leaves fell.

Conception

A child at the window sees her own growth
In houses across the snow, and leaps with hunger
To have here all at once the stupendous future.

But who, but who shall have it but the cell
At its creation in the ready womb
Where two together are multiplied by all,

And for an instant of outrageous joy
Advantages are known, from head to toes,
And all the flaming fingers are revealed

Even to this aching day when my decline
Is broken like a shell — O flaming bird.

All is conceived and multiplied by all —
Quick, before action takes the thought apart
And spreads it step by step along the life.

The Siblings

The tide left its lone few upon the beach — here four —
and went out with its other possibilities
drowned — all who hadn't happened lost in the sea
that cries at night with them, if numbers cry.

So we emerged and multiplied our cells
into ourselves and were arranged together
as we were for ourselves, are still a unit
that never can be sprung by all the world.

O stars, I think you are too many to utter
anything but One, the while the brothers and sisters
carry the characteristics of their difference
into the cells of sleep and death and sex.

Flower

I saw life as one flower moved by heaven
Of intensest sunlight to be whole and fresh,
Yes, fresh, the whole world fresh, its fabulous ages
Turned back into it as renewing sap.

Erect with disagreement from all directions,
Growing from the sun imbedded in the earth,
Extravagance of sex sustaining its fibres
Into all colours, it being never tired.

And in the night to ask what ultimate name
This flower has, what in a root tongue
I strain, I strain —
Would it be known if others
In the great field were known,
Comparison made
And nearer bright names given?

Autumn Stairway

The leaves are the floor of the wood, the rest is shape,
the little new things that hold their own, green, crisp and elate,
of delicately traced, small, having made a sedate
small contribution to the dying. Berries are plentiful
bright on the bush tips or blue.

The dogwood has all its shapes, the vine that clambered
upwards gone woody and thick as a wrist hangs in spaces
where props must have been once, twisted and spiralled,
tripping what I don't know, for the form is the thing now
sustained by the strength itself with hollows for loopholes.

The shadows come quickly to these and the day is left clinging
here and there in the trees, a blaze or a brilliant
pale light caught on a branch, and shed thoughtfully downward.
The leaves in this paleness spread are highly particular
fallen as they may be, open-faced in their waning colour
proclaiming their shapes as a study, 'What did I come from?'

The vine stem big around as an arm and become so woody
that it rises clasped around nothing where a trunk perhaps has fallen
makes a shape in the woodland of loop and labouring spiral
more spiritual than a straight trunk, out of leaves that have fallen
spiralling on up like a disengaged stairway.

Canoe

The canoe is one of the forms I was made to fit early
sitting still when I couldn't swim as the only safety,
and gradually, being advanced, learning to swim separately
and later taking over with the paddle, especially when alone
so land and water became sensibly one.

A form for moving around is seen lying
flush on the beach in the very early morning
to be pushed down among reeds
and let accept the water underneath   steady as a table
on the glassy whispering surface of the river.

Form fundamental of what does not stay
as long as spirit moves   it is away
and yet coheres   and whispers as it goes
on scintillating water at the bright sunrise.

And far upon an island shore pulled up
can stay and let the weather collect
about a form so ranging and exact.

From a River Boat

I saw out the open doorway of the hold
the river writing a page
line on line   this is a way to read

Here it seems that to move
through wrinkles of running water is to be all we need

The sun is not shining   the wind
is only enough to set up little waves

To be absorbed in this writing   in this silvery word
is to by-pass identity it has seemed
to be all the way composed
in a quiet meditation obliquely told

Look too at the water to see an outlook of history
a written page flowing along into fresh impulse
here charging the surface of words the silent and spoken records
and the wind turning the lines into another outburst

Travellers

This car of the long train lurches abreast
Of one on the next track and jolts to rest,
And here through ages in my mind I stare
Into that opposite car till I seem there,

Till I am here amidst the dirt and straw,
Having to peer out, press and moo and paw:
So unexpectedly I am with them
I lose the privilege from which I stem.

After shared ages we are parting, they
For the stockyard, I on my holiday;
We slide apart in our so separate cars —
I turn to look, they bawl between the bars.

Fall

Night and the apple found being large and generous
a full-blown one, a fragrant, fallen with the proverbial thud
and no wind in the late evening. Christ does no better than this.

Broken from the tree bough and whacking its way down
in the rustle of many branches ... darkness embraces
in the low place beneath where the chill grass is.

The fall of the freed apple the earth stops soundly
as moon fallen cold to the wet grass, the shadow,
to the cold drenched grass and the solid shadow,
and the thud says Land, land the arrival.

Moon Piece

A piece of the moon sits on a pedestal
and turns around to our gaze as the moon never has
in the blaze of light upon it to make it ours—
this silvery fist-sized portion of the ultimate moon,
a kind of anchor to pull it out of its usual position,
heavy, they say, though you can't tell with the glass on.

We are now the more ethereal and the moon less so
except that she leaves what we have in our hands and goes on
rolling around in our conception of how she should be
shining profound over the nature of the city
and over the country—we are used to ourselves in her distance,
it is almost as though the fingers had slipped.

The moon still trusts only what is left
and moves about our earth at her due distance
and says she'd rather be visited by a silvery path
she lets down over the fields heavily frosted.

And the piece remains a bit withdrawn in its closeness
a bit frosty and alone on its turning pedestal
a bit sophisticated and lost for the gaze of children.

So each goes differently on its own course
with components more than we knew hitherto, perhaps
a waiting wealth of moon for a cold night.

One

We are women in a cold hallway.
All our hearts beat quickly and our breaths,
Shallow with shock, draw sharply. On this day
Very close to us came one of the world's deaths.

She whom it came too close to weeps alone.
She will not have us with her; she asks God
Why it was hers, hers, hers, why like a stone
Her child lies — hers, hers of all the world.

Out of ourselves they come to us and our fears
Go with them always. Now her fears for him
Are done. We bow in pity, but our tears
Have in them thankfulness it was not ours.

Not ours, not ours. Beneath our sorrow sing
Our secret hearts — 'Not mine ... tonight I set
All places at my table, and I bring
To each pillow a special tenderness'.

The Great Activity of Death

I.

On one side feel a mass of the unknown
and on the other so much known
that it seems banked up as the forgotten,
banked up and stifled with its enormity it weeps and hugs.
This is no station and no journey
this is at the end of things, the unbelievable.

This is spasmodic as one going to sleep and returning
to awareness and going—blotting out; quite abruptly
the feverish hand cooled under mine, flattened out,
fire left the fingers late—curling almost to the last
they showed how vital was the hand.

The age-old question stands the same, for though I watched each moment
and held the very bones to beyond existence
all seemed enigmatical; I look back now for meaning
in the clear cut and poignant gestures: the immortal Gnome is left
an earthy thing treading the stairs still
calling up for Pix—'Is Pix upstairs?'

'Come   come   come   come   hurry   hurry   hurry   hurry'
Was it just the end he was inviting, or some healing or some glory?

Huddled up he turned his face away—
but I turned it to me just as it fell into the lines of death.

2. Waste

Human dignity is not what it looks like from outside
it resides in the waste
it spreads and anoints the uniter with a curious grace.

So the last spasms and the last air going out have a sigh sound
simple as wind at the eaves perhaps   who can know
who can know the support of arms to the disintegrating as he goes
and elbows his way out and bows
to all he has been when the fingers no longer close
on the holding hand
                              and on the crooked shoulder of hard bone
hangs the dilapidated   and the withdrawal
goes hand in hand with his into tomorrow.

3. 'You Know My Views'

I have tried to feel into his going
how it must have been with him
and perhaps with all who are not going
to a preconceived sphere of welcome
but for whom the ceremony is all of leaving.
How broadly staged it is, how unclouded by design
bare and naked of all but what happened.

Can I say this is completed by the clasp of the hand
and the fingers falling loose only after the within is crowded out?
Holocausts of humans have confirmed this act
and yet it breathes no sighs said once before.

4. Hold

The hands seem the last to give up — isn't it strange
they keep going at some perhaps destructive task
undoing something that is done, but busy and vaguely assertive
and holding on hard to the hand that is given them
so they when they let go are least assertive
unkind seeming by their previous kindness in keeping going.

But because he acted to the limit of his responsiveness
a small scene was allowed to be carried out
a ceremony of decease that was bit by bit
disposed of and laid away, the hands, the breath,
last words of 'no more' were only for the broth,

the small tangents of being went on bit by bit,
ease in them held decorously to the last —
small ceremony of leaving that the women sensed,
being able to put themselves on a level with the dying flesh.

A practised hand of love to the last instant
holds on   curls up   about the holding fingers,
answers the pressure even as the drifted
mind and its wreckage of body goes, releases
only at last the long time-lingering fingers
So fades the day   so pass away the years.

5. Mine

'Mine' he said of the special coverlet I had brought,
of anything he owned, not wanting it touched
guarding for when he would lie exposed to anyone's act.
But after he had said 'No more' he ignored all that
burrowed and left the empty thought.

I do not know what went then and what before
only that there was some grasp to his fingers
that had by then been loosened   and then none —
or was it as after writing a long poem
the fingers only held the afterthought
flimsy and vague and easily given up.

6. Breath

The last bits of air lingering in the lungs
supported two sighs
the two sighs of death
a sound not unfamiliar for the simplest distress
of strain, of love
carrying out the last release of breath.
This is the last air in that abandoned place
where the breath was concentrated as the soul of speech.

Let out they vanish and there is no more for him
to be regretful with, to wish the days again
to wish them back and better loved
and handled like treasures beyond belief.

7. Reach

He kept himself attached as long as possible
as though something life-giving would flood in —
love that though it would not save the life
supported it to the last wave
helped him accost a love that perhaps could reach
into some perspective, some fanciful hands underneath,
at least like falling asleep after pain
in the arms that wanted for him the best
so that time had some perspective
if not in continuance then in waves and repercussions
which are the same thing spread out
spread wide being what is the greatest and can abide.

A Marvel

One of the images in my brain
is a galaxy seen through a telescope years ago
at a distance from where my life is now,
small light blur becoming only in thought one of the great views

One of the views that can be looked at from another time
so distance lays out a plan   full of light   full of expansion
expanded back into itself and condensed
into one of the great grounds of sense

Only in thought is it realized
as more than a white breath   an enterprise in itself
where further laws are likely to be the same laws
to hold poised the great exuberance

And on and on to convert its size
into an intensity as immense   an action as intense
and governable in ways as ours
or how does it follow the heavens and yet can be recalled
to the telescope again even at this hour?

By time   years ago it was first seen
it has settled itself into the laws of dream
for the laws are the same
for inventing the telescope's eye as being in the brain

they light and relight   in inexhaustible profusion the sources of energy
a note of profoundest proportion earns them the name

More and more goes on and surrounds
the eclipsed self as the galaxy proves
in one of the great views   given of light
on the vast horizon of being
at the outskirts of all we don't have   do have and marvel at

The Shack

When travelling   I kept seeing   an occasional
shack   on the mountainside   clinging

When travelling I would see it   and go by
with it still in my thoughts no matter what next
and my sorrow for it somehow clinging and remembered

It was the shell   for a form of life   I apprehended
when travel is done and the language of life
and the beat of the landscape   give back the self

                              and passing by
I thought of shells each the same   and different

That was when I travelled   and now here
in the mountain hut   hear the wind go by
and the rain come so close that it is here
and the snow covers all

This is the hut of life   the tarred boards
echoing the rain   supporting the snow-cloud

giving themselves to a domain that has little other word
than the wind bringing down the leaves at the window

An echoing kind of place where I dwell now
remembering sometimes any passing sorrow

Losses in Blue

One being the loss of my sister   I catch on blue
the colour of her eyes   as belonging to me
search for it all over the place

and take it personally
in edges of fields and woodlands
in flower star and bell

in blue vetch   bluebells   blue flags   blue-eyed grass
in water divided by cloud forms from the blue above
in the small opening of forget-me-nots
in the deeps of sky blue amongst clouds

in shadows of a snowy winter such as we knew
shifting on glaze under a cloudless day

especially now in the very early morning
deep through the near bough and held till faded

She went out to California and wore dark glasses
against the singeing of the sun to which she was sensitive
That was long ago   and her eyes have closed since

nothing closes like blue about the woods and fields
in morning glory on the vine
in flower star and bell

Rocker

Rocking is so little   it only gains ascendancy
by going back to the trees in the forest

they rock too   and have within them
the same rings of promise
          of years to come as years accumulated

but these at home are cut on the bias   aslant and show
        a human attitude in design   and go
back and forth   slowly   bringing on the scene

things come and gone   the design is finished

       polished
persistent as that in the forest
             creak

and the sons returning   from death in childhood
come into the scene   as Grandmother rocks
and the hours   hold the years wanted
           back   forth   onward

The trees sway in the forest and their rings
are the design from which the rocker repeats
its catechism   the catechism within it

The Poets of Home

I in my age am sent
the poems of the dead
who are melted down to themselves

who lie in the thin wafers
who are holy and consumed for love

who are back in their time
who are in their native land
or journeying to return

They are over and done with
so they can return to be
the next people's splendour

I envy them their breath that is not
I envy them no tomorrow
I envy them the poem grown like a flower
that shall be picked by everyone
that passes   and the native
land of their dust

To the Sun in Age

How good will you be to what courts you still   asks your pardon
for absence of more graces   asks your instruction
for loving still the light hours   asks your forgiveness
for not providing the maximum of life where you lower yourself
asks your understanding:

that I stay   more than a branch
more than fruit, more than a petal even   more than pollen
or is it pollen that I hope to be besides another moment
so accepting the light that it looks good on the thinned skin
of such being   and the exposed vein   running its course

Sitting in the sun
seeing change more stressfully than in any other way
seeing the skin and the vein
drenched in sunlight like the flesh of — flash
a dive into the river of light
or long-ago islands or pregnancies
mounding the earth   from those years back

Now I no longer feel anything owed me   and the light is benign
that allows the moments to stay
aslant on the withering skin   intense

The sun is everywhere and at any age
or stage of life it may be intimately had
and at this time
lights the contortions of the veins
running under the skin   but in their stress
seeming to have the ways that conceive
of being like the mind   a leaf
Responsible as a leaf I compose something

About Dorothy Roberts

Some poets spend their youth surrounded by family who consider
writing for pleasure an act of eccentricity or rebellion, but this was
hardly the case with Dorothy Mary Gostwick Roberts. Born in
Fredericton, New Brunswick, on July 6, 1906, she was the daughter
of Theodore ('Thede') Goodridge Roberts and the niece of Charles
G.D. Roberts. Those brothers along with their cousin Bliss Carman
formed their clan's best-known trio of writers well into the twentieth
century, but another sibling of Charles and Thede, Jane Elizabeth
Gostwyke MacDonald, was also a poet, and her father had privately
published a booklet of her poems as far back as 1885. In 1899 she
appeared, along with Thede and their brother William, in *Northland
Lyrics*, a three-poet volume edited by Charles. It's clear Dorothy
Roberts was born into an environment characterized by both
parental and sibling support for writing poetry.

Before her birth, her father had lived briefly in New York with
his brothers Charles and Will and in Tampa, Florida, then travelled
to Cuba as a correspondent covering the Spanish-American War.
After catching malaria, he returned to Fredericton with the strong
possibility of dying from the disease, but was brought back to health
with the attentive help of a nurse named Frances Seymour Allen.
After he lived for two years in Newfoundland, published his first
prose romance and briefly joined his brothers again in New York, he
married Frances. During a two-year-long sojourn in Barbados, their
first child, Goodridge Roberts — later a significant mid-century
Canadian painter — was born, a couple of years before Dorothy.
Between 1905 and 1908, the young family often changed residences,
trying out flats, farmhouses and country cottages.

Thede wrote several books of poetry but was more prolific as the
author of adventure, historical romance and war novels, publishing
thirty-four over a span of twenty-nine years. Between 1909 and 1923
the restless family lived in England, France, rural New Brunswick by
the junction of the St. John and Oromocto Rivers, again in England
(where Thede was chosen by Lord Beaverbrook to work in the
Canadian War Records Office), Fredericton, Ottawa and the
Gatineau Hills. By Dorothy's late teens the family was back in
Fredericton, where she attended the University of New Brunswick

61

from 1926 to '28, briefly reported news for the Fredericton *Daily News*, and began selling poems and fiction to literary magazines. Just as her grandfather Roberts had made her aunt Elizabeth's work available to readers, Thede encouraged the publication of Dorothy's slim first volume of poetry, *Songs for Swift Feet*.

The same year that her chapbook appeared in the Ryerson Chapbook Series, Dorothy applied to Connecticut State College, where she soon met August Leisner. Eleven years older than Dorothy, he held a B.A. from Yale and an M.A. from Columbia. They married in early 1930 in Fredericton, and lived in Connecticut until 1937; their daughter, Anne, was born in '31, and son, John Bliss, in '37. During the Depression, cutbacks at the college deprived August of his job, then the couple lived until late 1940 in central Canada, where August completed a Ph.D. at the University of Toronto with extensive work on Charles G.D. During the second half of the 1930s, Dorothy's father was also living in Toronto, working as a newspaper columnist and editor.

Dorothy Roberts and August Leisner ended their years of Canadian residency in 1940, when August assumed a teaching position in Ithaca, New York, and worked on the production of army textbooks. Five years later, he was hired by Pennsylvania State University in State College (University Park), where the poet and her husband lived for the remainder of their lives. Over the following decades she wrote short stories and placed them in magazines, in part to supplement the family income, and completed a novel that was never published. In the 1950s she returned to writing poetry, publishing in journals such as *Hudson Review, Yale Review* and *New Orleans Poetry Journal*, as well as, in Canada, *Canadian Forum, Dalhousie Review* and *Queen's Quarterly*. In Pennsylvania she became active leading poetry discussions, giving readings and participating in literary festivals.

After the 1927 chapbook of her early poetry, three decades passed before the Ryerson Chapbook Series released a second brief volume of Dorothy's work, *Dazzle*, published in 1957 and dedicated 'To T.G.R.' (Thede had died four years earlier.) On the heels of *Dazzle* came another chapbook, *In Star and Stalk*, then Dorothy's first full-length collection, *Twice to Flame*, appeared in 1961, followed six years later by the collection *Extended*. Dorothy and August's daughter, Anne, died of cancer at the age of 57 in the later 1980s. August died in 1973 and did not live to see his wife's final two publications, *A Self of Loss: New and Selected Poems* (1976) and, two years before her own death, *In the Flight of Stars* (1991).

Poems by Dorothy Roberts appeared in anthologies such as *The Oxford Book of Canadian Verse, Made in Canada* and *Poetry by Canadian Women*, and despite her years living in the United States all of her collections were published in her native country. *The Essential Dorothy Roberts* is the first book publication of her work in the 21st century.

Dorothy Roberts: A Bibliography

As Gostwick Roberts:

Songs for Swift Feet (chapbook), Ryerson Press, 1927.

As Dorothy Roberts Leisner:

'Seven Poems.' In *Modern Canadian Poetry*, ed. Nathaniel A. Benson, Graphic Publishers, 1930.

As Dorothy Roberts:

Dazzle (chapbook), Ryerson Press, 1957.
In Star and Stalk (chapbook), Emblem Books, 1959.
Twice to Flame, Ryerson Press, 1961.
Extended, Fiddlehead Poetry Books, 1967.
The Self of Loss: New and Selected Poems, Fiddlehead Poetry Books, 1976.
In the Flight of Stars, Goose Lane Editions, 1991.